The · Life Cycle · Series

The Life Cycle of a
FROG

Bobbie Kalman & Kathryn Smithyman
Illustrated by Bonna Rouse

Crabtree Publishing Company

www.crabtreebooks.com

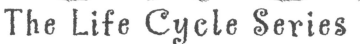

The Life Cycle Series
A Bobbie Kalman Book

Dedicated by Kathryn Smithyman
**For my husband, Steve Cruickshanks,
and for David, Erinn, Kevin, Joel and Tracy**

Editor-in-Chief
Bobbie Kalman

Writing team
Bobbie Kalman
Kathryn Smithyman

Editors
Amanda Bishop
Niki Walker

Computer design
Kymberley McKee Murphy
Margaret Amy Reiach

Production coordinator
Heather Fitzpatrick

Photo researcher
Heather Fitzpatrick

Consultant
Patricia Loesche, Ph.D., Animal Behavior
Program, Department of Psychology,
University of Washington

Photographs
Animals Animals: Zig Leszczynski: page 22
Marc Crabtree: page 30
James Kamstra: pages 18, 20, 27
Robert McCaw: pages 4, 8, 9, 13, 14, 16, 17, 19 (bottom),
    23, 26, 29 (top)
Joe McDonald: page 15
A.B. Sheldon: page 28
Tom Stack and Associates: Kitchin & Hurst: title page;
    Ryan C. Taylor: page 21 (top)
Michael P. Turco: pages 6 (top left), 7, 19 (top left and right),
    21 (bottom)
Other images by Adobe Image Library, Digital Stock, and
Digital Vision

Illustrations
All illustrations by Bonna Rouse except the following:
Barbara Bedell: series logo
Margaret Amy Reiach: front and back covers, pages 16, 17
Tiffany Wybouw: pages 4, 7, 8, 26 (top), 27 (left)

Crabtree Publishing Company
www.crabtreebooks.com   1-800-387-7650

PMB 16A
350 Fifth Avenue
Suite 3308
New York, NY
10118

612 Welland Avenue
St. Catharines
Ontario
Canada
L2M 5V6

73 Lime Walk
Headington
Oxford
OX3 7AD
United Kingdom

Cataloging in Publication Data
Kalman, Bobbie
  The life cycle of a frog / Bobbie Kalman & Kathryn Smithyman;
illustrated by Bonna Rouse.
    p. cm. -- (The life cycle)
    Includes index.
  Describes how frogs develop from eggs to adult frogs
and tells why some frogs are endangered and what individuals
can do to help protect them.
    ISBN 0-7787-0651-6 (RLB) -- ISBN 0-7787-0681-8 (pbk.)
    1. Frogs--Life cycles--Juvenile literature. [1. Frogs.
2. Tadpoles.]   I. Smithyman, Kathryn. II. Rouse, Bonna, ill. III. Title.
  QL668.E2 K343 2002
  597.8'9--dc21
                                        2001037214

Contents

 # What is a frog?

A frog is **cold-blooded** animal.
Its body temperature changes
as its surroundings change. For
example, the frog above raises its
body temperature by sitting in the
sun. If the frog gets too warm, it
can jump into cool water to lower
its body temperature. The body
temperature of a **warm-blooded**
animal, such as a dog, stays about
the same no matter how hot or
cold its surroundings are.

Double life

Frogs belong to a family of animals called **amphibians**. The word "amphibian" means "double life."

An amphibian lives part of its life in water and the other part on land. There are three main groups of amphibians: **anura**, **caecilia**, and **caudata**.

Frogs belong to the anura group. Anura means "no tail."

Caecilians have no limbs and look like worms.

Newts and salamanders are caudatans. This caudatan is a newt.

Fascinating frogs

Frogs have been on Earth for at least 190 million years! Today, there about 2,800 **species**, or types, of frogs. They live everywhere on Earth, except Antarctica. Most frogs live in swamps and rain forests. They cannot live in or near salt water.

The frog shown top left is an Asian leaf frog. The small frog on the flower is a reed frog. The three frogs above are tree frogs. Tree frogs have suckers on their toes that stick to slippery branches and leaves.

Many shapes and sizes

Frogs come in all colors and sizes. Shape and color helps some frogs hide from **predators**. The horn frog above easily blends in with fallen leaves. Poisonous frogs, such as the poison dart frog on the right, do not have to hide. Their bright colors warn enemies to stay away.

In water and on land

Almost all frogs live on land near ponds, streams, or rivers. They live on land because they breathe air, but water is very important to frogs, too! Frogs are born in water, and they return to it as adults. They need water to keep their thin skin from drying out. The green frog below is a common frog that lives in the **wetlands** of North America

Some frogs, such as this wood frog, get water without living near a pond. These frogs live in holes in the ground or in rotting logs. They find water in puddles or trapped in piles of leaves.

What is a life cycle?

All animals go through a set of changes called a **life cycle**. They are born or hatch, and then they grow and change into adults. As adults, animals make babies of their own. Most babies look like small copies of their parents when they are born.

A frog does not look like its parents when it hatches. It hatches from its egg as a **tadpole**. It then becomes a **froglet** and, finally, an adult frog. The frog's body changes completely during the four stages of its life cycle, shown below. This total change in its body is called **metamorphosis**.

frog eggs

tadpoles

From weeks to a year

All frogs go through metamorphosis, but some take much longer than others to become adults. Some frogs go through the four stages of their life cycle in a few weeks, but others take months. For example, it takes a whole year for a bullfrog to grow from a tadpole into an adult frog!

Life span

A **life span** is not the same as a life cycle. A life span is the length of time an animal is alive. A life cycle is the set of changes the animal goes through to become an adult that can make babies.

frog

froglets

Floating eggs

Each spring, a new life cycle begins as frogs lay their eggs. Frog eggs are called **spawn**. Most spawn is found in calm, shallow water. It sticks together in clumps of up to 4,000 eggs. Only about half of the eggs will hatch. Many will be eaten by turtles, fish, and other animals. Even if an egg does hatch, the tadpole may be eaten before it becomes an adult. Frogs lay a lot of eggs to make sure that at least some of their young will survive and grow into adults.

What's in an egg?

A frog egg starts out as a tiny, clear blob with a black spot in the middle. The black spot is the growing tadpole. The clear jelly is the "shell" of the egg. It protects the tiny tadpole and helps keep it warm.

A poison dart frog's eggs are so tiny that they can grow in a puddle on this leaf in the rain forest.

Teeny tiny tadpoles

A tadpole **hatches,** or breaks out of its egg, after about a week. It is now in the second stage of its life cycle. The tadpole's body is made up of a small head and tail. The tadpole has **gills** for breathing underwater, just as fish do. A tadpole is not a good swimmer when it first hatches. It sticks to floating weeds or grasses for several days after it hatches until it is strong enough to swim.

These young tadpoles cannot leave the water because they cannot breathe air with their gills. Soon they will grow lungs, however, and then they will start to breathe air.

Getting stronger

As the tadpole grows, it starts to swim farther and eat tiny water plants. When the tadpole is about four weeks old, skin starts to grow over its gills, and lungs grow inside its body.

When its lungs are ready, the tadpole swims to the surface of the water to breathe air. It grows tiny teeth that help it eat larger plants, as shown above. It begins swimming around with other tadpoles in search of food.

 # Growing legs

A tadpole eats plants almost nonstop, and grows quickly. As it grows and changes, the tadpole may even begin eating dead bugs, although most of the nutrients it needs are stored in its tail.

Within a few weeks, the tadpole's body, head, and tail are much longer than they were when the tadpole hatched. The tadpole above will soon form a neck between its head and body.

Growing legs

By the time a tadpole is nine weeks old, its body goes through even bigger changes. It sprouts hind legs—one on either side of its tail. Soon after that, it begins growing front legs where its gills used to be. As its legs grow, its tail begins to shrink.

The tail actually disappears into the tadpole's body! As the tail gets shorter and shorter, the tadpole begins using its back legs and **webbed** hind feet for swimming. The skin between the frog's toes allows the feet to act as paddles. The tadpole is now starting to look like a tiny frog.

Little froglets

This froglet is now a **carnivore**. It will eat only live insects and other **prey** for the rest of its life.

By the time a tadpole is three months old, its tail is almost gone. It is only a small stub. The tadpole's skin looks and feels like that of an adult frog. In fact, the tadpole looks like a miniature version of its parents. It is called a **froglet**.

Out of the water

With its new legs, a froglet can crawl out of the pond. It spends some time on land looking for food. When it was a tadpole, it used its tiny teeth to grab food, but as a froglet, it has a long sticky tongue for catching insects.

All grown up

A froglet becomes a frog when its tail is completely gone. This change can take a few days or weeks. At this time, its skin colors and markings are fully developed. The adult frog can **camouflage** itself by controlling the shade of its skin. It can stay warm by making its skin color darker and cool by making its skin a lighter shade.

The red-eyed tree frog hides its bright legs and toes by folding them under itself. The frog on the left is an eared tree frog that lives in Borneo in Southeast Asia.

An adult leopard frog's skin gets lighter or darker to blend in with its surroundings.

The cycle continues

Frogs **mate**, or make babies, in the spring. When a male frog is ready to mate, he heads for a pond, swamp, or even a puddle. Hundreds or thousands of other males join him. They wait for female frogs to arrive at the **breeding site**.

Frogs often breed in a pond that has calm water. They avoid ponds with a lot of fish because several types of fish eat small frogs and frog eggs.

The picture above shows several leopard frogs, gathering at a breeding site.

Picky about the pond

Many frogs use any suitable pond as a breeding site, but some frogs breed only in the pond where they hatched. These frogs **migrate**, or travel, back to the same breeding site every year. In most cases, their trip is fairly short, but some frogs travel several miles.

"Look at me!"

Male frogs sometimes compete for the attention of the females. They puff up their throat sacs and make loud croaking or chirping sounds. Females follow the sounds of males when they are interested in mating. Large frogs have deeper voices than the smaller frogs of their species. Female frogs prefer the deeper voices.

The green tree frog is also called a bell frog because the male's mating call sounds like a loud ringing bell.

Some poisonous frogs, such as these strawberry poison frogs, perform a dance to attract a mate. Since they are poisonous, the frogs do not need to worry about attracting the attention of predators.

Frog food

A frog hunts by waiting for live prey such as insects to fly by so it can snatch them with its long, sticky tongue. The frog's tongue is attached to the front part of its mouth. It reaches a long way, and it moves quickly.

Small frogs eat a lot of tiny insects. Large frogs eat rats, mice, and small snakes. Some large frogs, such as the frog above, even eat smaller frogs! Frogs have huge mouths that open wide in order to swallow large prey whole.

Watch out!

Like all animals, frogs are an important part of a **food chain**. They eat animals such as insects and, in turn, are eaten by other animals. Snakes, birds, fish, lizards, and rats all need frogs as part of their diet, or they may starve. Frogs also eat lots of insects—they help control pests naturally!

Surviving winter

Frogs cannot live in very cold temperatures. Frogs that live in places with cold winters must find somewhere to stay warm until spring arrives. They swim to the bottom of ponds and **burrow**, or dig, into the mud. The mud is warmer than the water or air and makes a good place for the frog to **hibernate**. To hibernate means to stay very still, as in a deep sleep.

Cosy and warm

Mud and plants on the bottom of the pond trap air bubbles, which frogs breathe. When the sun warms the pond in the spring, the frogs wake up and crawl out of their hole.

Avoiding heat

Frogs that live in hot areas also burrow and sleep to survive the heat and **droughts**, or lack of rain. Their sleeplike state is called **estivation**. It is similar to hibernation.

After the frog has crawled out of its burrow, it is very hungry and eats as much food as it can find.

Frog ...

Toads are a type of frog. They go through the same life cycle as frogs do and, like frogs, toads come in all sizes and colors.

A toad's body is slightly different than the bodies of other frogs. Look at the frog below and compare it to the toad on page 27.

A frog's bulging eyes allow it to see in front, beside, and behind at the same time!

Frogs do not need to drink water. They absorb it through their thin moist skin. A frog will die if its skin dries out.

A frog's long hind legs and webbed feet are perfect for jumping and swimming.

. . . or toad?

Most toads live in dry places. They have bumpy skin, whereas frogs have smooth skin. Toads have poison glands behind their eyes to protect them from predators. Their short hind legs are for hopping and walking—not for jumping.

Unlike frogs, toads such as this giant toad cannot change the color of their skin to camouflage themselves.

Frogs in danger

Frogs are very sensitive to their surroundings. Even tiny changes in the environment can greatly affect their health. Frogs are an **indicator species** because they react to these changes sooner than other animals do. The presence, absence, and health of frogs in an area can tell us about the health of the environment.

People all over the world are noticing **malformed** frogs, or frogs with abnormal bodies. Some of these frogs are missing eyes and legs. Others have extra or poorly formed legs. No one is sure why the frogs are becoming malformed, but many people believe that air and water pollution are to blame.

Scientists around the world are studying frogs to find out why they are malformed and dying. After eating malformed frogs, other animals are becoming sick, too. If pollution is making frogs and other animals unhealthy, it could also make people sick.

Fewer places to live

Frogs are part of a healthy planet, but they are in trouble. The greatest danger to frogs is the loss of their **habitats** all over the world. People drain wetlands, clear forests, and build roads and buildings where frogs once lived. They **introduce**, or bring new animals, into frog habitats. Some of these animals eat tadpoles and frogs, and others compete with frogs for food.

Frogs can survive only in water that is not polluted by chemicals. If there are no frogs or other amphibians living in a pond, it is a sign that the pond is polluted.

Vanishing frogs

The number of frogs is shrinking worldwide. At least three types have become **extinct** in the last twenty years. Extinct animals no longer live anywhere on Earth. Even rainforest frogs have begun to vanish, and they are in areas far from where people live. Scientists think that pollution may be to blame.

No sunscreen for frogs

Each year, more **ultraviolet light** from the sun reaches Earth. Ultraviolet light causes suntans, sunburns, and skin cancer in people. Some scientists think that the extra ultraviolet light may harm frogs as they grow and cause them to become malformed.

Helping our frog friends

You can help frogs and other animals by taking care of the environment. Ask your parents, teacher, or neighbors to help you organize a clean-up of local wetlands, such as ponds and streams. Picking up garbage near ponds and streams helps keep frog homes safe.

Ask your family and neighbors to stop using chemicals on their lawns and gardens. When it rains, the chemicals we spray on lawns and farms get washed into the ponds, rivers, and lakes where frogs live. These chemicals can hurt frogs and other animals.

These children are cleaning up a wetland area by collecting tires and other garbage.

Hidden chemicals

Even soaps such as dishwashing and laundry detergent have harmful chemicals in them. If your friends and family switch to natural or **biodegradable** soaps and cleaners, fewer chemicals will get into the water cycle. Remember that everything we spray on lawns, flush down toilets, or pour down sinks ends up in our lakes, ponds, rivers, and oceans!

Get hopping!

Check out the website **allaboutfrogs.org** for more information on helping frogs. At this website you can also learn how to raise your own frog!

Glossary

biodegradable Describing something that can be broken down naturally, without polluting

camouflage (n) Skin colors and patterns that help an animal blend in with its surroundings; (v) To blend in with one's surroundings

carnivore An animal that eats only meat

gill A body part found in fish and tadpoles that takes oxygen from water

habitat The natural place where a plant or animal is found

nutrients Materials needed by a body to grow and stay healthy

predator An animal that hunts other animals for food

prey An animal that is hunted by another animal

webbed Describing feet with thin sheets of skin between the toes

wetlands Areas of land that are under shallow water some or all of the time

Index

1 2 3 4 5 6 7 8 9 0   Printed in the U.S.A.   1 0 9 8 7 6 5 4 3 2